Make It!

Making Music

Rebecca Sjonger

AV2
www.av2books.com

Step 1
Go to **www.av2books.com**

Step 2
Enter this unique code
UTXCIIOUX

Step 3
Explore your interactive eBook!

AV2 is optimized for use on any device

Your interactive eBook comes with...

Contents
Browse a live contents page to easily navigate through resources

Audio
Listen to sections of the book read aloud

Videos
Watch informative video clips

Weblinks
Gain additional information for research

Slideshows
View images and captions

Try This!
Complete activities and hands-on experiments

Key Words
Study vocabulary, and complete a matching word activity

Quizzes
Test your knowledge

Share
Share titles within your Learning Management System (LMS) or Library Circulation System

Citation
Create bibliographical references following the Chicago Manual of Style

This title is part of our AV2 digital subscription

1-Year 3–8 Subscription
ISBN 978-1-7911-3306-1

Access hundreds of AV2 titles with our digital subscription.
Sign up for a FREE trial at **www.av2books.com/trial**

Making Music

CONTENTS

Time to Make!

What do the ancient Greeks and the superstar disc jockey, or DJ, Deadmau5 have in common? They are all makers! The link between them is one of the world's most popular ways of making music—keyboard instruments. More than 2,000 years ago, the Greeks invented an organ powered by water. Later makers replaced the water with air to make pipe organs. Skip ahead to today and Deadmau5's prized grand piano. He hooks it up to his computer to make electronic music. Who will design the next advance in keyboards? It could be you!

Pioneers of Music

Throughout history, the pioneers of music have been creative and resourceful. In ancient Sri Lanka, someone joined a coconut shell and a bamboo stem with a few other everyday objects. It became one of the earliest instruments to be played with a **bow**. People still make music using ordinary items today. The members of Vienna's Vegetable Orchestra are an example. They make and play vegetable instruments—from carrot flutes to pumpkin drums. Could coconuts or carrots be used in your music projects?

The Maker Movement

People who invent new instruments and ways of performing music are part of a growing group called makers. They are from many different fields, but they have a lot in common. Makers often collaborate, or work together, in makerspaces and labs. They gather to share tools and knowledge. There might be a makerspace near you.

Risk-Taking

Hands-on experiments are a big part of the maker movement. Makers take risks because they believe they can change the world. Failure will not stop them. They learn from their mistakes and persist until they find solutions. Creative resources and inspiration are everywhere.

Design Processes

Some people make their own instruments because they are expensive to buy and repair. Other makers have an instrument they want to adapt. They alter the original design to work in a different way. Music makers bring their ideas to life through a variety of creative processes. They may design by trial and error. This process involves trying different approaches until one works well. Often makers start with an idea, develop a **prototype**, test it, and then improve it.

The Science of Sound

Believe it or not, when makers innovate with music they also experiment with physics. This science explores how energy and **matter** interact. Did you know that sound is actually energy that can be heard?

Vibrations to Sound

When an artist such as Taylor Swift strums her guitar, she causes its strings to vibrate. The matter that surrounds the strings—air in this case—begins to vibrate, too. Vibrations produce sound waves that travel in all directions.

*Even modern electric guitars still rely on vibrations to make sounds.

Hearing

The outer ear collects sound waves. These waves move through the ear canal and hit the eardrum. Its tightly stretched tissue vibrates like the surface of a drum. Parts in the inner ear pick up the vibrations and send signals to the brain. It interprets them and we hear sounds. If someone tells you to turn down the music on your headphones, listen to them! Loud sounds can damage the inner ear and cause hearing loss.

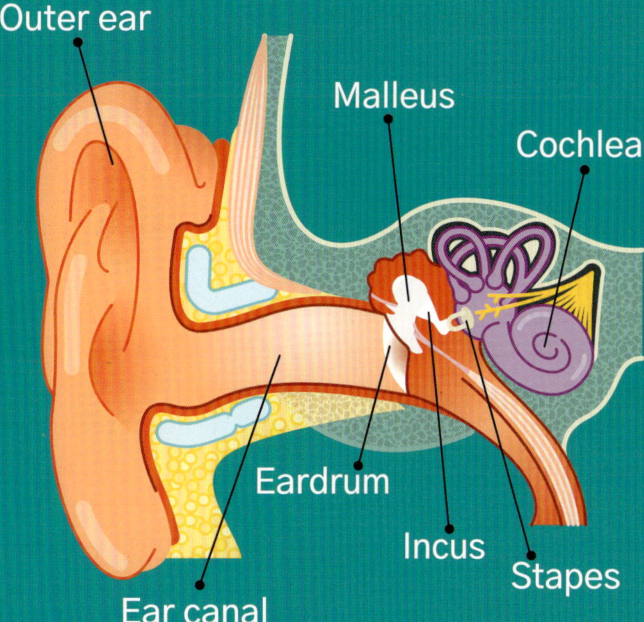

Make Some Noise

Any object that vibrates creates a sound that could become music. You can try it right now! Clap your hands or stomp your feet to produce vibrations. Tap on a glass or slam a door shut. Grab a pen and drum a beat on a variety of surfaces. The very first instruments began with people using everyday items to make sounds. Challenge yourself to make as many unique sounds as possible with objects you find in your kitchen.

Feeling Sounds

After German composer Ludwig van Beethoven lost his hearing, he sat on the floor and played a legless piano. He could not hear his own music, but he could feel the piano's vibrations through the floor. People who are deaf can enjoy music by touching an instrument while a musician plays it, or feeling vibrations coming from speakers.

The Sound of Music

Mixing random sounds together just makes noise. We create music by purposely combining sounds. Understanding a few main sound concepts will help you with making your own music.

Pitch

The speed of vibrations affects sound. Faster vibrations have a higher **pitch**, whereas slower vibrations sound lower. Each musical note links to a pitch. Mariah Carey is famous for her wide range, which is the span of notes she can sing. Her range is no match for a pipe organ, though. Each pipe has a different pitch and one organ may have hundreds—or thousands—of pipes.

Timbre

What happens if a variety of instruments play the same pitch? They will not sound the same. Our ears pick up subtle differences in the qualities of sound produced by each instrument, known as their **timbre**.

Volume

The intensity or size of sound waves affects volume. The crowd at a Drake concert perceives the vibrations blasting from speakers as having a louder volume. If he whispers to someone onstage, however, the low intensity lowers the volume. These sound waves are too quiet for others to hear.

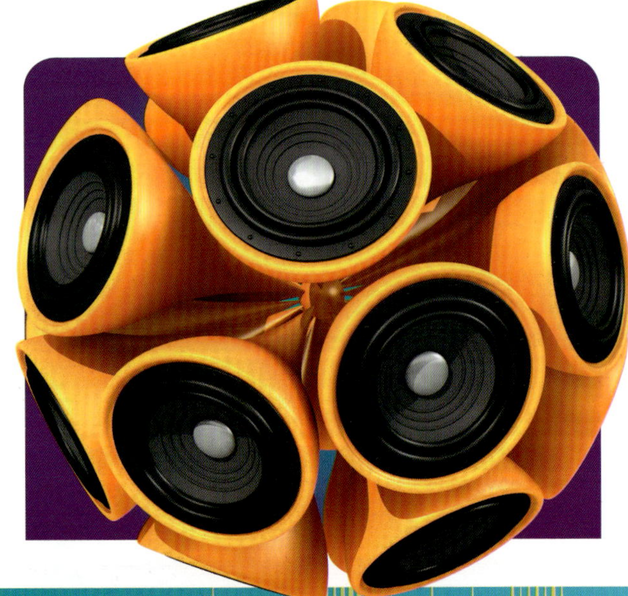

Changing Vibrations

When making your own musical instrument, consider how it produces vibrations and if you can modify them. For example, guitar strings have varying thicknesses, which create different pitches. Tightening, loosening, shortening, and lengthening the strings also adjusts their pitch. A guitarist changes notes by pressing down on the strings, which shortens them. The size, shape, and material of a guitar will also affect its timbre.

Iner Souster

Most people would regard a broken speaker, fridge parts, and an old bowl as trash. Toronto-based musician Iner Souster (born 1971) saw the makings of a large string instrument that he later named the bowafridgeaphone. His first attempt to create the instrument ended in disaster when he pulled a string too tightly and the whole thing fell apart. He did not give up—he just tried again until he was successful. He started making at age 12 when he pieced together old parts he found in his dad's garage. He has made many one-of-a-kind musical instruments since then.

Make It!

Water Trombone

Some instruments produce vibrations by having air blown through a tube. The length and width of the tube determine the pitch. The materials used to make the instrument affect the timbre. The volume changes with the strength of the blowing.

You Will Need

- A tall drinking glass or bottle
- Water
- A drinking straw

Step 1

- Fill the glass or bottle with water. While holding the top end of the straw,insert it into the water.

Step 2

- Line your lips up with the top of the straw so that when you blow, your breath moves across the top opening of the straw. It should produce a sound.
- If you do not hear a sound, change the placement of the straw or try pressing it against your bottom lip.

- Lower the straw into the water until the top part of the straw is just above the top of the bottle and blow.
- Keep blowing as you slowly raise the straw up through the water.
- Try quickly moving the straw up and down. Notice how the pitch changes.
- Test what happens when you blow softer or harder on the straw.

- Now make some music! Create a simple **melody**, which is a series of high and low notes, on your water trombone.

Conclusion

- What did you observe about pitch and volume while playing your water trombone?
- How did the pitch change as the amount of air in the straw increased or decreased?
- In what ways did blowing harder or softer change the volume?

Make It Even Better!

Try this activity again. Experiment with using different materials, such as other liquids, or straws with varying diameters and thicknesses. You could also try it with multiple straws cut at different lengths. How do you think changing the materials will affect the pitch or volume of your water trombone?

Vibrating Air

Water trombones—and brass trombones—are part of a huge group of instruments that make sounds mainly by vibrating the air inside them.

One, Two, Three, Blow!

Many thousands of years ago, people blew air into hollow animal bones to make music. Covering a carved finger hole changed the pitch, just as it does on flutes today. Simple whistles made from bones were another early instrument that relied on vibrating air. They played one note but could increase in volume with stronger blowing.

There are now hundreds of instruments that make sounds by vibrating air. Harmonicas, bagpipes, and even conch shells belong to this diverse group. Along with designs and materials, the way the air is blown, and how strongly, will affect volume and pitch. A player's lips may buzz against a mouthpiece, as with a tuba. Lips may also vibrate directly on an object, such as the opening of a conch shell. Other instruments, including clarinets, involve blowing air over one or more **reeds**, which changes how the air vibrates.

Experiment with vibrating air! What sounds can you produce with a cardboard tube, wind-up siren, or party horn?

*The way a trumpeter blows changes how the air vibrates inside the instrument.

Sax Hacks

Saxophones are less than 200 years old. This makes them new inventions compared to most instruments. They are named after their maker, Adolphe Sax, who was born in Belgium and started making instruments at about age 14. Like many music makers, Sax enjoyed mixing different parts of instruments together. When he put the reed mouthpiece of a clarinet onto a tuba-like brass body, he designed the first saxophone, or sax.

Inventive makers will **hack** any instrument—even newer ones like the sax. Angel Sampedro del Rio made the first bamboo sax in 1985. He used trial and error to perfect the sax in his family's workshop in Argentina. The final design joins bamboo stems together. It uses traditional reeds, but the bamboo body gives the instrument a distinct timbre.

Vibrating Strings

How many ways can you think of to vibrate the strings of a musical instrument, such as a guitar? In addition to strumming strings, musicians can pick, pluck, strike, and move a bow across them.

So Many Strings

The idea to stretch strings tightly to create sounds is ancient. One of the earliest examples is the harp. Egyptians in 3000 BC used hair or plant fibers as harp strings. Centuries later, lyres were popular string instruments in Greece. Their strings were made of dried sheep intestines! A piece of horn or bone was used to pluck the strings to vibrate them. People still play harps and lyres today. Other modern string instruments include the banjo, cello, and mandolin.

Did you know that vibrating strings also make the sounds inside pianos? Pianists press keys that connect to small hammers. These hammers hit the strings and make them vibrate. Each key plays a different note because each string has its own pitch. Pressing a key softly or powerfully changes the volume of its sound.

Super Strings

We have pianos because of Bartolomeo Cristofori. This Italian inventor played about with the design of the **harpsichord** for years. This led to him making the first piano around 1700. At the same time in Italy, Antonio Stradivari and his family were handcrafting string instruments such as violins. Their artistry made them one of the most famous families of makers ever. A Stradivarius instrument sells for millions of dollars today.

If Cristofori or Stradivari were around today, they could try new technologies such as three-dimensional (3D) printers. Find out if a library near you has one of these printers. You can watch as it "prints" layers of material, such as plastic, to create objects from drawings. 3D printers can even make the bodies of string instruments!

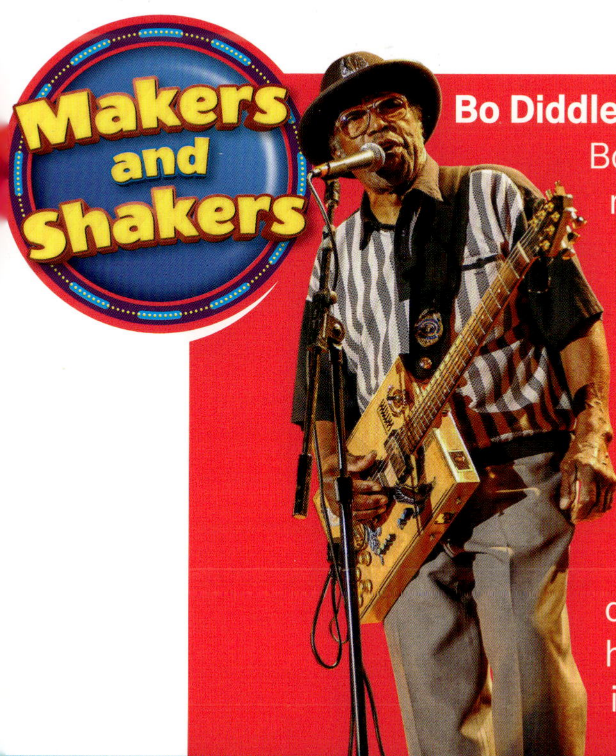

Bo Diddley

Bo Diddley (1928–2008) was a maker who ruled rock and roll in the 1950s. Friends used to call him "the junkman" because he made instruments from just about anything. He even filled plastic toilet parts with black-eyed peas to make maracas! His signature creations were rectangular guitars made from old wood and cigar boxes. Diddley did not just invent instruments—he rocked with them. His style still influences music today.

Vibrating Instruments

Strings are not the only part of an instrument that can produce vibrations. One group of instruments vibrate all over their bodies. Depending on the materials used to make them, they can have different pitches or one distinct sound.

Shake, Rattle, and Roll

The people who created flutes with animal bones also made music by striking or scraping bones together. Using different objects, such as stones or body parts, produced other sounds. These early makers also strung together seeds, shells, and other everyday items to create bracelets and anklets. They rattled when the wearers danced. People also made music with items such as dried gourds, a type of fruit. The **friction** between the outer gourd and the hardened seeds inside it caused sound vibrations. You could make similar musical instruments yourself!

The discovery of metals allowed makers to create sounds that people had never heard before. These instruments were also more durable. Bronze bells that date back about 4,000 years still exist in China. Modern metal instruments in this group include cymbals, triangles, and xylophones.

Making Old Things New

American inventor Benjamin Franklin tried his hand at making a vibrating instrument in the 1700s. People already knew that moving a wet finger around the rim of a glass created vibrations and a beautiful sound. Franklin built on that idea. His armonica used dozens of glass bowls that spun as a single unit. In your own music projects, consider how you can use old ideas to make something new!

Vibrating instruments do not require complicated designs like that of Franklin's armonica. Music makers are resourceful. They can produce sounds from almost anything. For example, the musical saw is exactly what you think it is. A musician carefully holds a metal handsaw and pulls a bow across it or taps it with a hammer to create vibrations.

Vibrating Membranes

Instruments that vibrate relate closely to instruments with vibrating **membranes**. In fact, they are often lumped into one group called percussion instruments. However, they make sounds differently.

Membrane Materials

A vibrating membrane is a tightly stretched material that usually covers the opening of a drum base. The earliest membranes were skins from animals such as elephants and alligators. As they dried, the skins tightened over the openings of hollow clay or wooden frames. Ropes often held the edges of the membranes against drums.

After thousands of years, a new membrane material replaced animal skins. An American chemical company invented the first synthetic drumhead in the 1950s. It was more durable and less prone to damage when damp, which was a problem with animal-skin drumheads.

Drumsticks

At first, musicians used their hands to vibrate membranes. Wooden tools fall apart over time, so it is difficult to know who made the first wooden drumsticks. They are at least 1,000 years old, though. Using different drumsticks changes the sound of a drum. The vibrations vary depending on their tip shapes and the woods used to make them.

Modern Instruments

Common drums played today include timpani, bongo, bass, snare, and tom-tom drums. Like earlier drums, modern versions often have wooden bodies, also called shells. Makers also use metals and plastics to create drum bodies. The different materials produce different sounds. The shape and thickness of shells and drumheads also change the timbre.

You can find drum-making inspiration from the prototype created by a team from Yamaha. They began the design process by brainstorming ideas for a drum kit. It needed to include drums, cymbals, and cowbells. They used their best ideas to design and build a prototype. They created a ball-shaped drum kit that the drummer stands inside.

Make It!

DIY Drum

Drums have distinct timbres based on their designs and materials. Experiment with materials and sounds by making your own drum!

You Will Need

- Cylindrical drum body materials, such as cardboard tubes or empty metal or plastic containers
- Durable drumhead materials, such as balloons, packing tape, or plastic lids
- Materials to attach the drumhead, such as elastic bands, staples, or duct tape
- Scissors

Step 1

- Brainstorm possible supplies for your drum. Consider items for the body that are different sizes and depths and have walls with varying thicknesses. These factors will decide the timbre of the drum, along with the drumhead you use.
- Select one body object and one drumhead material from your list of ideas.

Step 2

- If the drumhead will not stay on with the materials you have selected, experiment with other materials from your brainstorming session. Try different ways of attaching the drumhead. Remember, makers learn from failures instead of quitting when things go wrong.

- Use your fingers to tap a rhythm on your drum and hear how it sounds. You can adjust it by tightening or loosening the drumhead.

- Try out your new drum! See if it sounds any different when played on the ground or held off the floor between your knees. Test the drum in spaces with different **acoustics**, such as a large, carpeted room or inside a dry bathtub.

Conclusion

Observe whether your drum is able to make different sounds. For example, does it change when you strike various spots on the drumhead? Why do you think the size, thickness, and tightness of a drumhead changes the sound of a drum? Reflect on what other materials you would try working with if you did this activity again.

Make It Even Better!

Why stop at one drum when you can make a whole kit? Brainstorm a list of creative resources you could use to make more drums by varying the sizes, shapes, and materials. What are the pros and cons of your ideas?

Vibrating Vocals

There is one musical instrument that almost everyone has. It is not the product of brainstorming, prototyping, or testing. People use the original design in a huge variety of ways. It is the human voice! When you speak or sing, air causes two tiny folds in your throat to vibrate. Try humming with your fingers on your throat to feel the vibrations.

Early Vocals

Evidence suggests that people once sang in cave areas where the acoustics made their voices sound the best. The sounds of the earliest vocal music are lost to us today. However, history shows that every culture has its own distinctive styles.

Vocal music has many different roots. For example, **yodeling** began in the Alps mountain range as a way to call out to faraway places. It turned into music over hundreds of years. Early choral singing in southern Africa enforced the values of the community. In traditional **throat singing**, Canadian Inuit women usually perform in pairs. They developed it as a pastime while men were off hunting.

*Opera is a theatrical form of singing. It has remained popular for more than 400 years.

Vocal Innovators

Modern music makers continue to invent new ways to use their voices. In the early 1900s, **scat singing** mimicked sounds made by instruments. It inspired later musicians such as Bobby McFerrin. He produced every sound with his own body!

McFerrin's music influenced **beatboxing**. People also call it vocal percussion because it sounds like electronic drum machines. Hip-hop artists, such as Jay-Z, often beatbox. Rap is another innovation that is even more central to hip-hop. It started in the 1970s as talking in rhymes to a beat. Is there a form of vocal music that you would like to try or adapt?

Electronic Music

Electricity has been widely available in North America for about 100 years. Thanks to this technological advance, the past century has been a busy one for music makers.

Going Electric

One of the first instruments to use electricity as part of its original design is the telharmonium. This early—and complicated—electric organ sent sound over telephone lines. It was also the first **synthesizer**. These machines make electronic versions of sounds produced by other instruments. The Original New Timbral Orchestra, or TONTO, is the world's largest synthesizer. Its makers collaborated over several years to combine many synthesizers into one instrument.

You can also use electricity to enhance traditional instruments. A common way is to add **pickups** to string instruments. They turn vibrations into electrical signals. **Amplifiers** send the signals to speakers, which send out sound waves. Guitarists playing many kinds of music, including metal, pop, and even country, use them to increase volume. Makers are also creating **augmented** traditional instruments, such as trumpets. These new versions have sensors that react to a player's movements. The slightest touch affects the sound and gives a musician precise control.

Mixing Music

When people refer to electronic music today, they mean music created on computers and audio technologies like turntables. The first DJ used records and audiotapes. They experimented by recording sounds, mixing them in new ways, and varying their speeds. Adding computers to their tools created new musical opportunities. Daft Punk, Skrillex, and other electronic music performers mix diverse songs and sounds to create high-energy performances. You can try it yourself by searching on the internet for online mixing programs.

Sydney Blu

Canadian DJ Sydney Blu (born 1977) shows off her music-mixing skills around the world. She and Deadmau5 played for 35,000 fans at one Toronto show! She bought her own turntables after seeing an electronic music show in college. Being a DJ may look easy, but Blu says it is a lot of hard work. DJs need to coordinate the beats of multiple songs in front of a live crowd. An interviewer from Garnish Music Studios asked Blu about her "fails." She replied, "There are never fails, only lessons!" That is the maker spirit!

New Vibrations

Makers are always looking for new ways to create sound vibrations. Some of their musical creations are so unique that they stand apart from the rest.

Bridges and Benches

Nothing is safe from a music maker with a great idea—not even a bridge. The sounds made by the Brooklyn Bridge in New York inspired Di Mainstone to create the Human Harp. A musician—or "movician"—wears a harness that attaches to the cables of a bridge. Electric inputs collect and record their sound vibrations to make music. The London-based artist now collaborates with others to play bridges around the world.

If you can play a bridge, why not play a bench? MIT's Media Lab created a small computer that translates data into music. Users interact with an everyday object that has sensors on it. Their movements change the pitch and volume of the music. Early prototypes used a ball of ice and a drinking fountain. Next, makers hacked a bench. Two people sitting on it touch copper plates on the armrests. Then they can hold hands, poke each other, or even kiss to produce unique melodies!

Vibrating Liquid

Have you ever heard of a hydraulophone? You may have played one without even knowing it. Often found in public spaces, they look like a cross between a water fountain and a piece of modern art. Vibrating liquid, usually water, runs through hydraulophones. Musicians adjust pitch by covering finger holes, which changes the liquid levels. Inventor Steve Mann has made hundreds of these instruments. He wants people to have fun as they play them. Consider adding some fun into your own music projects!

Make It!

Pegboard

Are you ready to make music? In this activity, challenge yourself to create as many musical sounds as possible on a pegboard-based instrument. Then, play some homemade harmonies!

You Will Need

- A pegboard or pinboard (the size depends on your ideas and plans)
- Pegs, hooks, string, and other fasteners
- Metal, plastic, and wooden household objects
- Elastic bands, clear fishing line, metal wires, and other strings
- A DIY drum

Step 1

- Begin by brainstorming ways to produce vibrations using materials attached to a pegboard or pinboard. List innovative ways household objects could vibrate or cause other things to vibrate.
- Review your ideas and select the ones that you think will work best.
- Draw plans of your space to make sure your ideas will fit.
- Start to add the pins or pegs to your board.

Step 2

- Make sure you will produce multiple pitches and timbres by including a wide variety of materials. Use pegs, hooks, string, and other fasteners to attach materials to your pegboard or pinboard. Varying widths and sizes of similar items will create a range of pitches.

Step 3

- Collaborate with a friend to come up with more diverse ideas. Test each part as you build your instrument. If it does not work as you expected, refine your idea.

Step 4

- Make as many pegboards as you like! Add items that can work as a maraca, drum, or chime, or include your drum from the earlier activity.
- After assembling your pegboard, play it! Invite a friend or family member to join you in making music.

Conclusion

Which parts of your instrument work best? How does their performance relate to the vibrations they make? What would you do differently if you redesigned your instrument?

Make It Even Better!

Consider what factors limit the sounds you make. How could you solve these issues? Improve your pegboard instrument by refining parts that did not work well. Experiment with new sounds and enjoy your making experience!

Test Your Knowledge

ONE	TWO	THREE
For how long has opera remained popular?	What tools did the first DJs use to make music?	Who invented the armonica?

FOUR	FIVE	SIX
What part of the ear collects sound waves?	When was Bo Diddley born?	What material was used to make the earliest drum membranes?

SEVEN	EIGHT
Where was Adolphe Sax born?	Where did yodeling begin?

ANSWERS

1. More than 400 years
2. Records and audiotapes
3. Benjamin Franklin
4. The outer ear
5. 1928
6. Animal skins
7. Belgium
8. In the Alps mountain range

Key Words

acoustics: the characteristics of a space that influence how sound travels around it

amplifiers: devices that intensify sounds by sending them as electrical signals to speakers

augmented: an instrument that has electronic modifications

beatboxing: producing sounds similar to a drum machine by using the human voice

bow: a long, thin tool used to vibrate the strings of an instrument

friction: the resistance caused by moving two or more objects together

hack: to rework an original object or idea into something new

harpsichord: a stringed musical instrument that has two keyboards

matter: something that has mass and occupies physical space

melody: a series of notes played in a particular order

membranes: thin layers of material

pickups: electronic devices that collect sound vibrations from an instrument and change them to electrical signals

pitch: a sound found on a scale of low to high

prototype: a physical model built for testing designs

reeds: thin slices of wood or metal in a mouthpiece that help vibrate air inside an instrument

scat singing: a form of vocal music in which performers imitate the sounds of instruments

synthesizer: a musical instrument that produces electronic versions of sounds made by other instruments

throat singing: a form of vocal music in which performers control their breathing to make sound vibrations

timbre: the distinct sound quality made by an instrument

yodeling: a form of vocal music in which performers switch between high-pitched and regular singing

Index

Get the best of both worlds.

AV2 bridges the gap between print and digital.

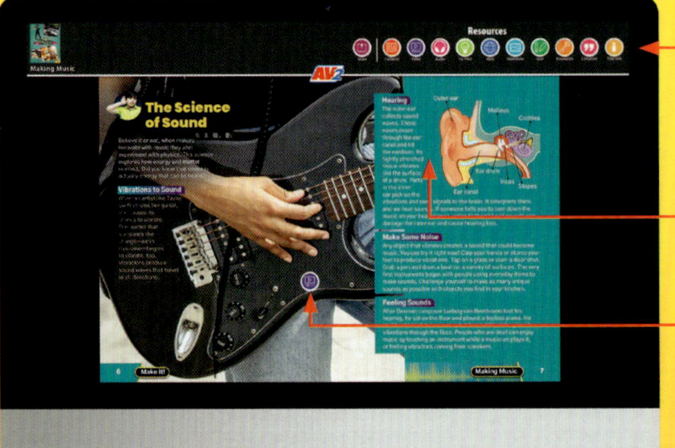

The expandable resources toolbar enables quick access to content including **videos**, **audio**, **activities**, **weblinks**, **slideshows**, **quizzes**, and **key words**.

Animated videos make static images come alive.

Resource icons on each page help readers to further **explore key concepts**.

Published by AV2
276 5th Avenue
Suite 704 #917
New York, NY 10001
Website: www.av2books.com

Library of Congress Cataloging-in-Publication Data

Names: Sjonger, Rebecca, author.
Title: Making music / Rebecca Sjonger.
Description: New York, NY : AV2, 2021. | Series: Make it! | Includes index. | Audience: Ages 10-14 | Audience: Grades 4-6
Identifiers: LCCN 2020001769 (print) | LCCN 2020001770 (ebook) | ISBN 9781791123567 (library binding) | ISBN 9781791123574 (paperback) | ISBN 9781791123581 | ISBN 9781791123598
Subjects: LCSH: Musical instruments--Construction--Juvenile literature.
Classification: LCC ML460 .S583 2021 (print) | LCC ML460 (ebook) | DDC 784.192/3--dc23
LC record available at https://lccn.loc.gov/2020001769
LC ebook record available at https://lccn.loc.gov/2020001770

Printed in Guangzhou, China
1 2 3 4 5 6 7 8 9 0 25 24 23 22 21

062021
101320

Art Director: Terry Paulhus Project Coordinator: John Willis

The publisher acknowledges Alamy, Getty Images, and Shutterstock as the primary image suppliers for this title.